YOUR KNOWLEDGE HAS VALUE

- We will publish your bachelor's and master's thesis, essays and papers

- Your own eBook and book - sold worldwide in all relevant shops

- Earn money with each sale

Upload your text at www.GRIN.com
and publish for free

Bibliographic information published by the German National Library:

The German National Library lists this publication in the National Bibliography; detailed bibliographic data are available on the Internet at http://dnb.dnb.de .

This book is copyright material and must not be copied, reproduced, transferred, distributed, leased, licensed or publicly performed or used in any way except as specifically permitted in writing by the publishers, as allowed under the terms and conditions under which it was purchased or as strictly permitted by applicable copyright law. Any unauthorized distribution or use of this text may be a direct infringement of the author s and publisher s rights and those responsible may be liable in law accordingly.

Imprint:

Copyright © 2017 GRIN Verlag, Open Publishing GmbH
Print and binding: Books on Demand GmbH, Norderstedt Germany
ISBN: 9783668514232

This book at GRIN:

http://www.grin.com/en/e-book/373224/strategy-planning-as-an-instrument-for-coordinating-affiliations

Jimmy Jimnah

Strategy Planning as an Instrument for Coordinating Affiliations

GRIN Publishing

GRIN - Your knowledge has value

Since its foundation in 1998, GRIN has specialized in publishing academic texts by students, college teachers and other academics as e-book and printed book. The website www.grin.com is an ideal platform for presenting term papers, final papers, scientific essays, dissertations and specialist books.

Visit us on the internet:

http://www.grin.com/

http://www.facebook.com/grincom

http://www.twitter.com/grin_com

Table of contents

1. Introduction 2
2. Mission 3
3. Vision 3
4. Objective 4
5. SWOT Analysis 4
     5.1 Strengthens 4
     5.2 Shortcoming 5
     5.3 Openings/ opportunities 5
     5.4 Dangers/ Threats 6
6. Versatile/ Adaptive Strategy 6
     6.1 Administration Delivery 7
     6.2 Bolster Components 8
7. Conclusion 9
9. Bibliography 10

1. Introduction

Strategic planning is an absolutely genuine and supportive instrument for coordinating an extensive variety of affiliations, including restorative administrations affiliations. The legitimate level at which the key arranging technique is relevant depends on upon the unit's size, its complexity and the partition of the organization gave. A cardiology division, a hemodynamic unit, or an electrophysiology unit could be an appropriate level, the length of their techniques change in accordance with various game plans at more raised sums (Rachel, 2012). The pioneer of each unit is the person in control to advance the whole procedure, an inside and major piece of his or her part (Peter & Vanessa, 2015). The system of essential arranging is programmable, deliberate, goal, and widely inclusive and fuses the short, medium and whole deal, allowing the human administrations relationship to focus on appropriate and persisting changes for what's to come.

2. Mission

Our social insurance association, a non-benefit, medicinal services affiliation, is set out to:

- Initiative and greatness in passing on quality medicinal services organizations

- Growing the horizons of restorative data through biomedical investigation

- Instructing and get ready specialists and other therapeutic administrations specialists

- Endeavoring to improve the wellbeing status of our gathering

- Quality persistent thought is our need.

Giving astounding clinical and organization quality, offering compassionate care, and supporting examination and restorative guideline are crucial to our focal objective.

3. Vision

- Draw in and update relationship with the most qualified, refined and respected specialists, scientists, medicinal orderlies, other human administrations specialists and staff

- Show impressive clinical quality, organization quality, and worth

- Foster a public of superb clinical and operational execution, and furthermore responsive and sympathetic thought

- Give perceived ventures and organizations of awesomeness that develop a tradition of clinical improvement, biomedical investigation, remedial guideline and gathering organization

- Stay at the bleeding edge of advances in arrangement and science through a strong, advancing obligation to biomedical investigation and restorative preparing

Give prevalent limits, workplaces, and advancement for the full continuum of social medicinal services organizations

4. Objective

1. To convey quality wellbeing administrations to the patient

2. Expanded open nature with the foundation.

3. Enhance linkages to the specialist's office board and in addition arranging.

4. Expanded nature with the work of the board for ceaseless selection of board people

5. SWOT Analysis
5.1 Strengthens

1. Electronic Health Record foundation

2. Biomedical Informatics venture and resources

3. Assistant structures foundation

4. Data Warehouse

5. High figuring limit

6. MyChart Patient gateway foundation

5.2 Shortcoming

1. Insufficient direct reimbursement organizations and wellbeing guideline, no state/government financing for high school pregnancy

2. High usage of weakened leave, pitiful routine with regards to wiped out leave guide, no registry contracts equal persistently high patient sharpness to medical caretakers extents

3. Make an effort not to offer routine arrangement of costs positions to be filled in cleft for understanding security

4. Poor movement arranging

5. Lose extraordinary agents because of political air

6. under spending design routinely

7. Difficult to discharge agents

5.3 Openings/ opportunities

1. Propel chip away at nursing is extraordinarily supported and progressed with educational cost reimbursement

2. Ability to work a grouping of jobs with relative effortlessness, both between institutions, states, and countries, without losing step or survey

3. Military game plans without work punishment

4. National and overall business

5. Nursing preparing programs

5.4 Dangers/ Threats

1. Genuine national human administrations reform will impact all parts of affiliation

2. Not ready to get best candidate due to long hold up time

3. Patients socioeconomics

4. More essential offers of patient working expenses go to uncompensated care than different doctor's facilities

5. Government specialist's office by and large records for more level of uncompensated thought costs.

6. Versatile/ Adaptive Strategy

Late examinations over the natural, money related, and humanistic systems have discovered that structures work in cycles of change and reestablishment (Michael & Thomas, 2015). To keep up their financial sensibility, focuses depend to changing degrees on tolerant charges, raising charges, and choosing guaranteed patients. Along these lines, free centers have not begun expenses (Rachel, 2012). In any case, we suggest amazing verbal showdown among free office and FQHC respondents for the need to build the charges or, with the desire of complimentary focuses, the unavoidable weakness to avoid some sort of cost structure (possibly in light of sliding scale, as required in FQHCs) (David & Rachel, 2016).Enrolling a higher rate of paying clients is a fundamental indispensable change for FQHCs and family arranging focuses. Most human services workplaces are moving a long way from guide fundamental thought organizations to concentrate on giving masses based focus open health. A office needs a pioneer who appreciates business—it's a business requiring affiliation, arranging and control. Most affiliations see the need to improve viability, nature of thought, and responsiveness to patients (Peter & Vanessa, 2015). A key piece of key responses is begin or fortifying of group situated relationship with private portion components, fusing associations with neighborhood medicinal services associations, appreciating penniless solution projects, and utilizing volunteers.

6.1 Administration Delivery

The goal of compassionate customer organization tends to basic qualities and execution of organizations that patients experience or see(Peter & Vanessa, 2015). The consideration is basically on factors that impact understanding slants and immovability and their point of view of clinical and organization quality. Eg: those segments that redesign, or discrete, as indicated by the customer, the affiliation's organizations from various providers offering practically identical administrations.

All correlated data and information are utilized to develop our affiliation's execution in giving quality therapeutic administrations. The target spotlights on improving social protection comes about, organization transport comes about, and viable status (Rachel, 2012). The target focuses on finishing preferred outcomes relative over various affiliations that pass on similar social protection organizations.

It actuates all staff to make and utilize their most extreme potential to the affiliation's objectives in the scopes of character, sensitivity, wellness, consistence and support. It joins each illustrative by putting extra discretionary effort and the likelihood of remaining undaunted and with the relationship for a drawn out extend of time (Peter & Vanessa, 2015). The work environment and air must help the success, headway and action of staff in order to fulfill full intrigue and execution unfathomability.

6.2 Bolster Components

It is anything but difficult to see how collaboration is essential for the conveyance of human administrations (Peter & Vanessa, 2015). Specialists, restorative overseers, medicate pros, specialists, and other wellbeing specialists must organize their activities to pass on protected and capable patient thought.

Information organization offers affiliations structure, some help with overseeing, and benefit by information by - diminishing dangers, extending efficiencies, finishing the upper hand (David & Rachel, 2016).

It is not astounding that overall population remains impassive in regards to quality measures that may gage a provider's steadfastness and reputation yet say little as to how its patients truly do (Rachel, 2012). The principle bona fide measures of significant worth are the outcomes that issue to patients. Additionally, when those outcomes are assembled and announced transparently, providers confront tremendous weight—and strong persuading strengths—to upgrade and to get best practices, with a few changes in comes about.

7. Conclusion

From the examination, unmistakably collaboration is a basic section of achieving high steadfastness for human administrations affiliations. HRO circumstances ask for collaboration and, consequently, the investigation of gathering get ready can give remarkable bits of learning and showed systems for improving execution inside such affiliations(Peter & Vanessa, 2015). All things considered, we endorse that social protection get footing from the more than 20 years of investigation on bunch execution and preparing and that these models be at first attempted and a short time later planned into the demonstration of therapeutic administrations and the preparation of wellbeing specialists (David & Rachel, 2016). Notwithstanding the way that this will take noteworthy time, possibly spreading over a time, this system has been one of the key drivers in various business ventures fulfilling the most hoisted reliability possible (Rachel, 2012). We assume that the challenges we have shown here outfit a guide with which social protection can continue. Finally, so as to accomplish the objective of the association the versatile system ought to be agreeable collaboration and less charges for persistent care. These procedures will take the upper hands.

9. Bibliography

Rachel Day " (2012), "Strategic Planning in Healthcare Organizations.Available at - http://www.revespcardiol.org/en/strategic-planning-in-healthcare-organizations/articulo/90147901/;

Peter D Jacobson, Vanessa K Dalton (2015), "Survival Strategies for Michigan's Health Care Safety Net Providers", http://www.ncbi.nlm.nih.gov/pmc/articles/PMC1361175/;

David P Baker, Rachel Day (2016), "Teamwork as an Essential Component of High-Reliability Organizations" http://www.ncbi.nlm.nih.gov/pmc/articles/PMC1955345/;

Michael E. Porter, Thomas H. Lee, MD (2015), "The Strategy that will fix health care", https://hbr.org/2013/10/the-strategy-that-will-fix-health-care;